17 Prehistoric Fishes

Everyone Should Know About

Stanton F. Fink

Volume V of Stanton's Coloring books

Acknowledgments

and Dedication

To my father, in whose books I discovered my first monsters.

To Will Caligan, whose help and encouragement is one of the primary reasons for this coloring book's existence.

To Bretton Carter, to whom I owe my sanity, if not life to in his helping to obtain certain references

To Professor Matt Friedman, whose correspondence over the years helped refine my pictures, in addition to his scientific descriptions of some of the species I've illustrated.

To my friends, who helped push me to make this.

Table of Contents

Introduction

The purpose of this coloring book series is to provide information on various prehistoric animals both profoundly famous and incredibly obscure to artists of all ages. Of course, there is a lot of material to work with, as animals have been a major component of Earth's ecosystems for at least 670 million years.

The term "fish" is fluid and awkward, even when used in a strictly taxonomic sense. One definition, the very crudest, is "any obligately aquatic animal that swims," which includes invertebrates, i.e., jellyfish, as well as chordates that we've been taught since childhood that are not fish, i.e., whales. For the purposes of this book, we will use a less crude definition where a fish is defined as "any obligately aquatic, gill-breathing craniate chordate that is not a member or descendant of Tetrapoda," so that we can also include hagfish, too.

Glossary

- **Aquatic**- Living in water.
- **Arthropod**- Any member of the animal phylum Arthropoda, including trilobites, arachnids, crustaceans, insects, myriapods and their relatives. All arthropods have armor-like, jointed exoskeletons made of chitin-derived plates, sometimes reinforced with calcium carbonate, and jointed limbs.
- **Cambrian**- A period of time in the Paleozoic Era from 541 to 485 million years ago.
- **Carboniferous**- A period of time in the Paleozoic Era from 359 to 300 million years ago.
- **Cenozoic**- An era of time in the Phanerozoic Eon from 65 million years ago until now.
- **Chordate**- Any member of the animal phylum Chordata, including sea squirts, lancet fish, and vertebrates (such as lampreys, sharks, tuna, frogs, lizards, chickens, and people). All chordates have, at least at some point in their life cycle, a notochord, a long, flexible rod, usually made of cartilage, or, in the case of most vertebrates, cartilage and bone, running down the back from head to tail, directly beneath the neural tube.
- **Cretaceous**- The last period of time in the Mesozoic Era, from 144 to 66 million years ago.
- **Crustacean**- Any arthropod of the Subphylum Crustacea.
- **Devonian**- A period of time in the Paleozoic Era from 414 to 360 million years ago.
- **Ediacaran**- The last period of time in the Precambrian Eon from 635 to 542 million years ago.
- **Eocene**- A period of time in the Cenozoic Era from 55 to 33 million years ago.
- **Fauna**- In an ecological context, "fauna" refers to the animal components of an ecosystem.
- **Formation**- In a geological or paleontological context, a formation is a group of rock layers.
- **Gnathostome**- A gnathostome is any vertebrate chordate with a moveable jaw (or had an ancestor with one).
- **Holocene**- A period of time in the Cenozoic Era from 12,000 years ago until now.
- ***Incertae sedis***- A Latin phrase literally meaning "uncertain seat." *"Incertae sedis"* is a term in classification used to refer to a species or group whose relationships with related organisms are unclear or poorly defined.
- **Jurassic**- The second period of time in the Mesozoic Era, from 199 to 145 million years ago.
- **Mesozoic**- An era of time in the Phanerozoic Eon from 249 to 66 million years ago.
- **Miocene**- A period of time in the Cenozoic Era from 23 to 5 million years ago.
- **Mollusk**- Any member of the animal phylum Mollusca, including snails, clams, squid, octopuses, tusk shells and chitons. Most mollusks have a calcium carbonate shell, and a toothed, file-like tongue called a radula. All mollusks have a cape-like organ, the

mantle, which usually secretes the shell, and houses breathing organs, and a nervous system.

- **Nekton**- Any aquatic animal that lives either entirely or almost entirely in the water column, and relies on its own swimming or propulsion abilities to keep and move itself in and around the water column. Anchovies, porpoises and ichthyosaurs are examples of nekton.
- **Neogene**- The second third of the Cenozoic Era, comprising of the Miocene and the Pliocene periods.
- **Oligocene**- A period of time in the Cenozoic Era from 33 to 23 million years ago.
- **Ordovician**- A period of time in the Paleozoic Era from 484 to 440 million years ago.
- **Paleocene**- A period of time in the Cenozoic Era from 65 to 55 million years ago.
- **Paleogene**- The first third of the Cenozoic Era, comprising of the Paleocene, Eocene, and Oligocene.
- **Paleozoic**- An era of time in the Phanerozoic Eon from 249 to 66 million years ago.
- **Permian**- The last period of time in the Paleozoic Era, the time of "The Great Dying," or most severe of all known extinction events, from 299 to 250 million years ago.
- **Pharynx**- A structure in the throat of many animals located directly behind the mouth or oral chamber. In vertebrates, it often houses breathing structures, like gills.
- **Plankton**- An organism that uses water currents and waterflow to as its primary means of transportation in the water column because it is either too small to move long distances by its own power, or lacks the ability to propel itself entirely. Sargassum seaweed and jellyfish are two varieties of plankton.
- **Pleistocene**- A period of time in the Cenozoic Era from 3 million years ago until 12 thousand years ago.
- **Pliocene**- A period of time in the Cenozoic Era from 5 to 3 million years ago.
- **Quaternary**- The last third of the Cenozoic Era, comprising of the Pleistocene and the Holocene periods.
- **Terrestrial**- Living on land.
- **Triassic**- The first period of time in the Mesozoic Era, from 249 to 200 million years ago.

Name   Haikouyu

Species	*Haikouichthys ercaicunensis*
Phylum	Chordata
Subphylum	Vetulicolia
Class	Vetulicolida
Family	Vetulicolidae
Size	2.5 centimeters
Time Period	"Stage 3" of the Cambrian Period, 515 million years ago
Location	Chengjiang County, Yunnan Province, China
Comments	*Haikouichthys ercaicunensis* is a slender, 2.5-centimeter long craniate from the Early Cambrian of Yunnan Province, China. To be more precise, it is from Haikou, near Ercaicun in Yunnan Province (not to be confused with Haikou of Hainan Province). In life, it would have probably resembled a freshly hatched salmon fry, with large eyes, and gillslits, but no pelvic or pectoral fins, no jaws, and no distinction between the dorsal and caudal fins. The living animal is thought to have traveled in large schools due to how fossil slabs contain numerous individuals trapped together in death.

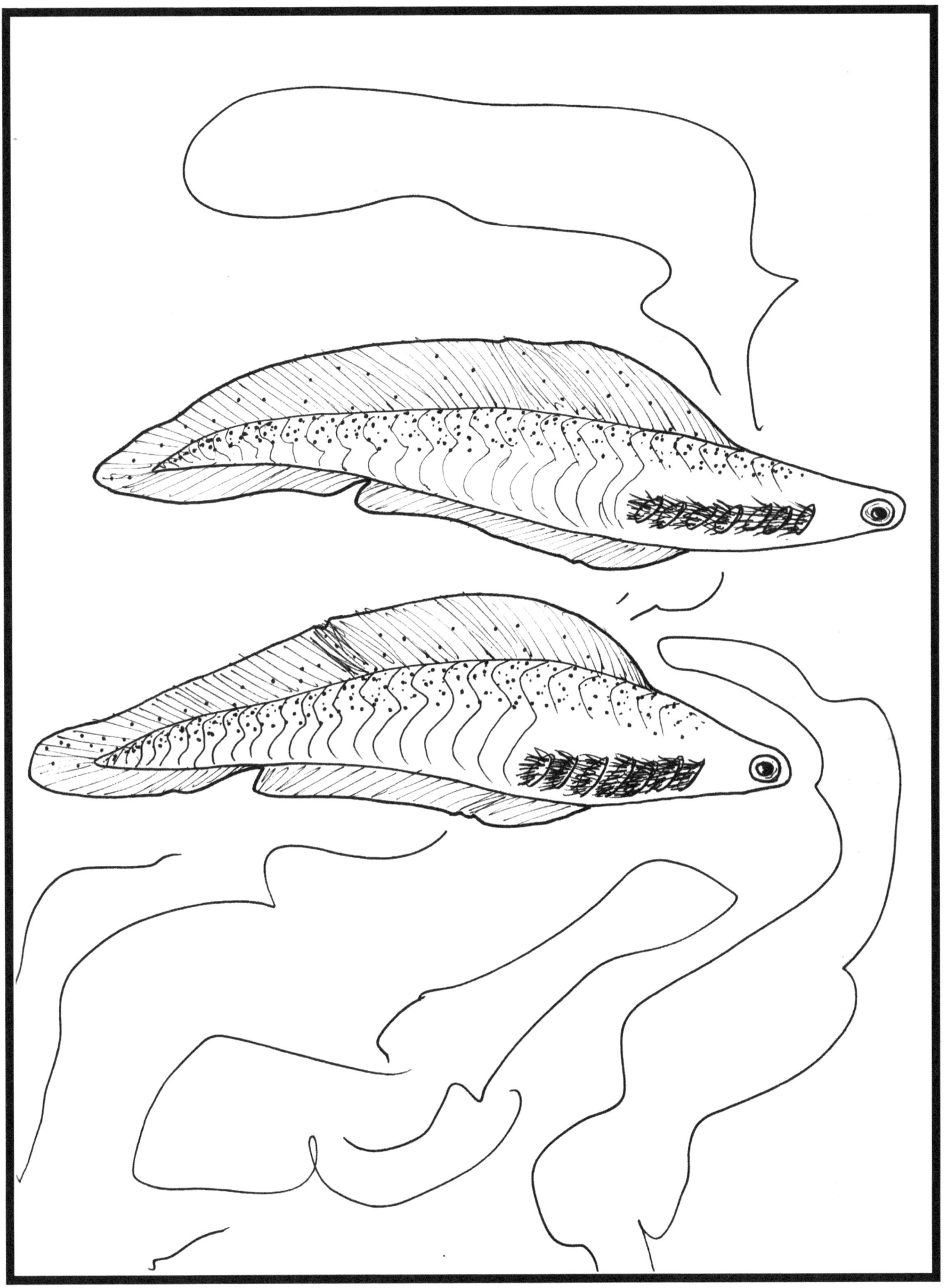

Name

Sacabamba Huq'ullu

Species	*Sacabambaspis janvieri*
Phylum	Chordata
Subphylum	Vertebrata
Class	Pteraspidomorphi
Subclass	Arandaspida
Order	Arandaspidiformes
Family	Sacambaspidae
Size	Average length about 25 centimeters
Time Period	From the Dapingian to Sandbian epochs of the Ordovician, 470 to 455 million years ago
Comments	The Sacabamba Huq'ullu, *Sacabambaspis janvieri,* is the oldest vertebrate known from whole, three dimensional fossils. While there are older vertebrates known, these older fossils are known from impressions, fragments, or flattened, carbon smears.

The huq'ullu is known from tear-dropped shaped fossils that suggest a tadpole-like animal that had an armored, egg-shaped body, and a long, whip-like tail. The tail had an upper fin-lobe, a lower fin-lobe, and a little fin at the tail tip. The eyes were located at the very front, directly above the mouth, and pointing forward like the head, and there was a pair of nostrils just below the eyes. The huq'ullu was a marine filterfeeder that lived in shallow coastal waters off the southern coast of Ordovician Gondwana.

Thirty fossil specimens were found near the village of Sacabamba, Bolivia. The arrangement of the fossils suggests that the living animals were clustered together when the group was killed in a traumatic event, where they were buried and suffocated by a flow of freshwater and debris caused by a rainstorm. Fossils of related species were found in Argentina, Australia, and Oman, leading researchers to realize that different species were found all along the coasts of Ordovician Gondwana.

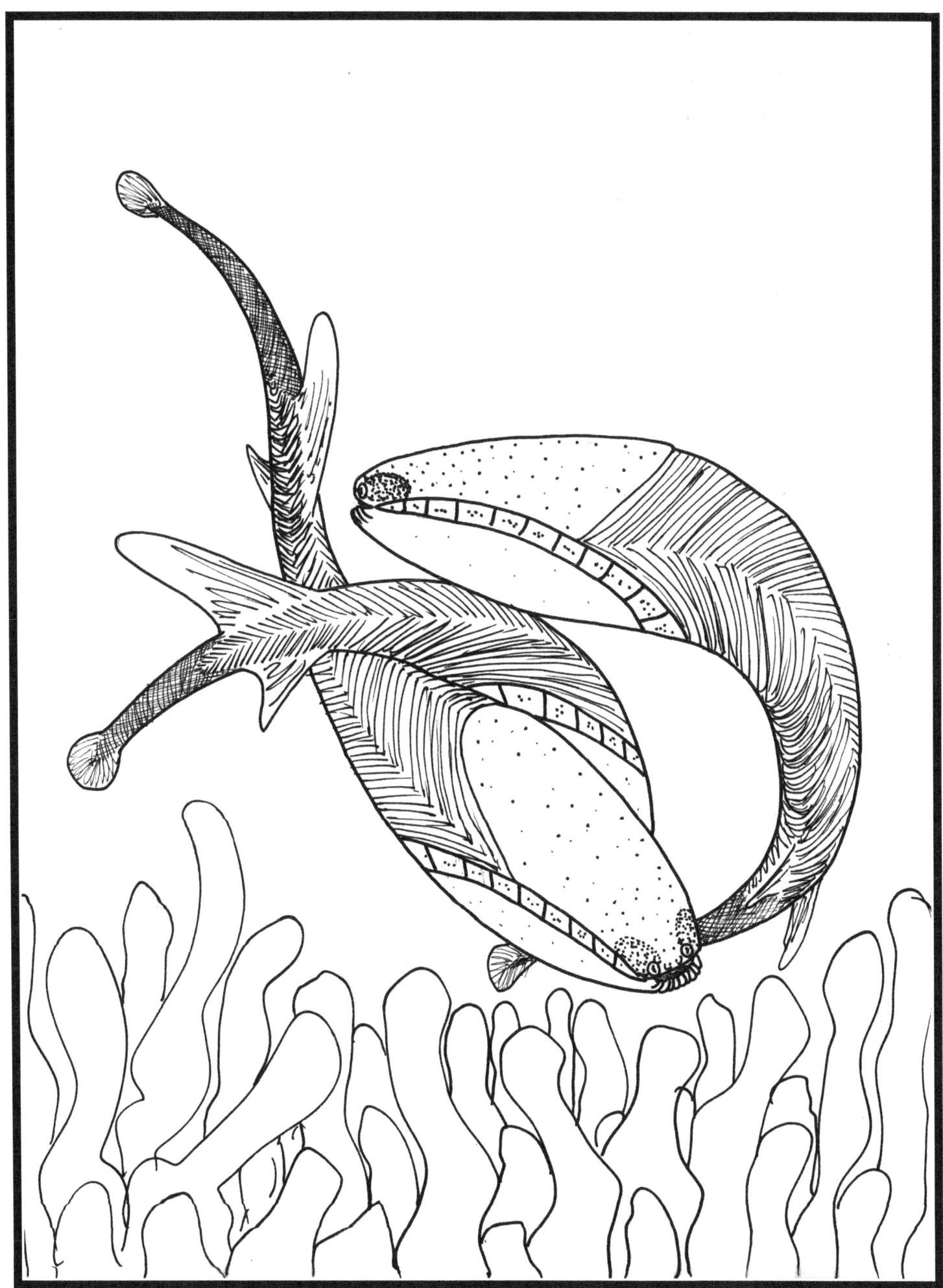

Name

Silurian Qilin

Species   *Qilinyu rostrata*

Phylum   Chordata

Subphylum   Vertebrata

Class   Placodermi

Order   *incertae sedis*

Size   Fossils about 12.6 centimeters long, living animal estimated to be at least 20 centimeters long

Time Period   Late Ludlow epoch of the Late Silurian, 419 million years ago

Location   Qujing, Yunnan Province, China

Comments   The Silurian Qilin, *Qilinyu rostrata*, is one of at least two Silurian-aged placoderms (the other being the Perfect Jawfish, that are thought to form a link between arthrodire placoderms, including the terrorfishes and *Wuttagoonaspis*, and "crown-group gnathostomes," including all jawed vertebrates from sharks to humans.

The anatomy of the snout and the jaws, which give the Silurian qilin a "dolphin-like profile," show basic features common to all jawed vertebrates, as well as giving researchers an idea of both snout (or maxilla) evolution in primitive gnathostomes, and of what sort of jaws the ancestral gnathostome had.

Lifestyle-wise, the Silurian qilin lives up to the classical placoderm stereotype of the bottom-dweller, as its upturned snout and flattened head and thorax strongly suggest a sturgeon-like animal that happily plowed through the substrate in search of edible goodies to nibble on or snap up.

Name	# Gemünden Rochen
Species	*Gemuendina stuertzi*
Phylum	Chordata
Class	Placodermi
Order	Rhenanida
Family	Asterosteidae
Size	30 to 100 centimeters in length
Time Period	Emsian epoch of the Early Devonian period, 407 to 393 million years ago
Location	Gemünden municipality, Rhein-Hunsrück, Germany
Comments	

Das Gemünden Rochen, *Gemeundina stuertzi,* is the best known and best-studied of the rhenanid placoderms, as it is the only rhenanid known from whole fossils. Because of the Gemünden rochen's beautifully preserved fossils, scientists know a great deal about its overall anatomy, to the point where *G. stuertzi* has become an iconic animal of the Devonian.

Fossils of the Gemünden rochen range from 30 to 100 centimeters in length: the largest specimen was originally described as its own species, "*Broilichthys heroldi.*"

Through the rochen's whole-body fossils, rhenanid placoderms are understood to have had flattened bodies, long tails, and broad pectoral fins similar to skates and rays of today. However, even though rhenanids are often compared to skates and rays, because of the rhenanids' upturned mouths, they would have been ecologically more similar to modern-day goosefish and stargazers, snapping up any animal that wandered too closely to their mouths. Unlike all other known placoderms, the rhenanids' armor were made of a mosaic of unfused scales that correspond to the plates of other placoderms.

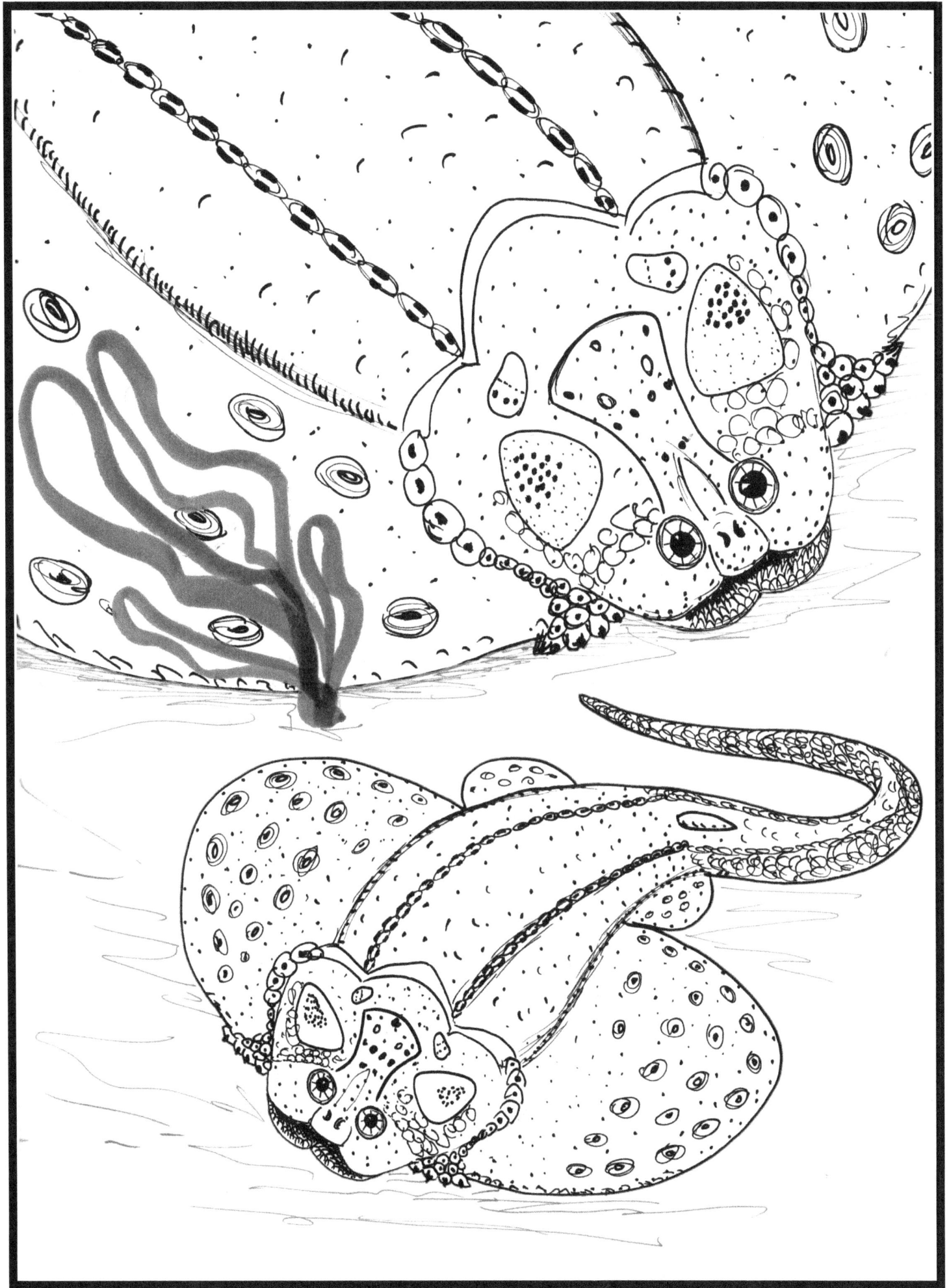

Name	Cannibaby
Species	*Delphyodontos dacriformis*
Phylum	Chordata
Class	Chondrichthyes
Subclass	Holocephali
Order	*incertae sedis*
Size	4 to 11 centimeters in length
Time Period	Middle Pennsylvanian epoch of the Carboniferous, about 300 million years ago
Location	Bear Gulch, Montana
Comments	The Cannibaby, *Delphyodontos dacriformis*, is a mysterious, teardrop-shaped relative of the chimaeras known only from about a precious few fossils, all of which are either of recently born juveniles, or of aborted fetuses, depending on their sizes. The adult form is currently remains unknown.

All of the fossils depict a tadpole-like animal, with a beak-like tooth-whorl. The largest specimen shows a spiny or prickly shagreen on the skin. The sharp tooth-whorl, coupled with traces of poop still in the digestive tract, strongly suggest that the cannibaby, like many modern-day sharks, practiced intrauterine cannibalism. Intrauterine cannibalism is either when the mother nourishes those of her unborn, developing offspring that have finished absorbing their yolksacs by secreting more unfertilized eggs for them to eat, or when more developed unborn offspring eat their smaller, less developed siblings, or both situations. During the Late Carboniferous, Bear Gulch was a tropical lagoon, and much like some tropical lagoons of today, had anoxic zones that killed or harmed the lagoon inhabitants. It is thought that the mysterious mothers of the cannibabies prematurely gave birth due to dying or becoming injured while travelling through these anoxic zones, which then also killed the cannibabies, themselves.

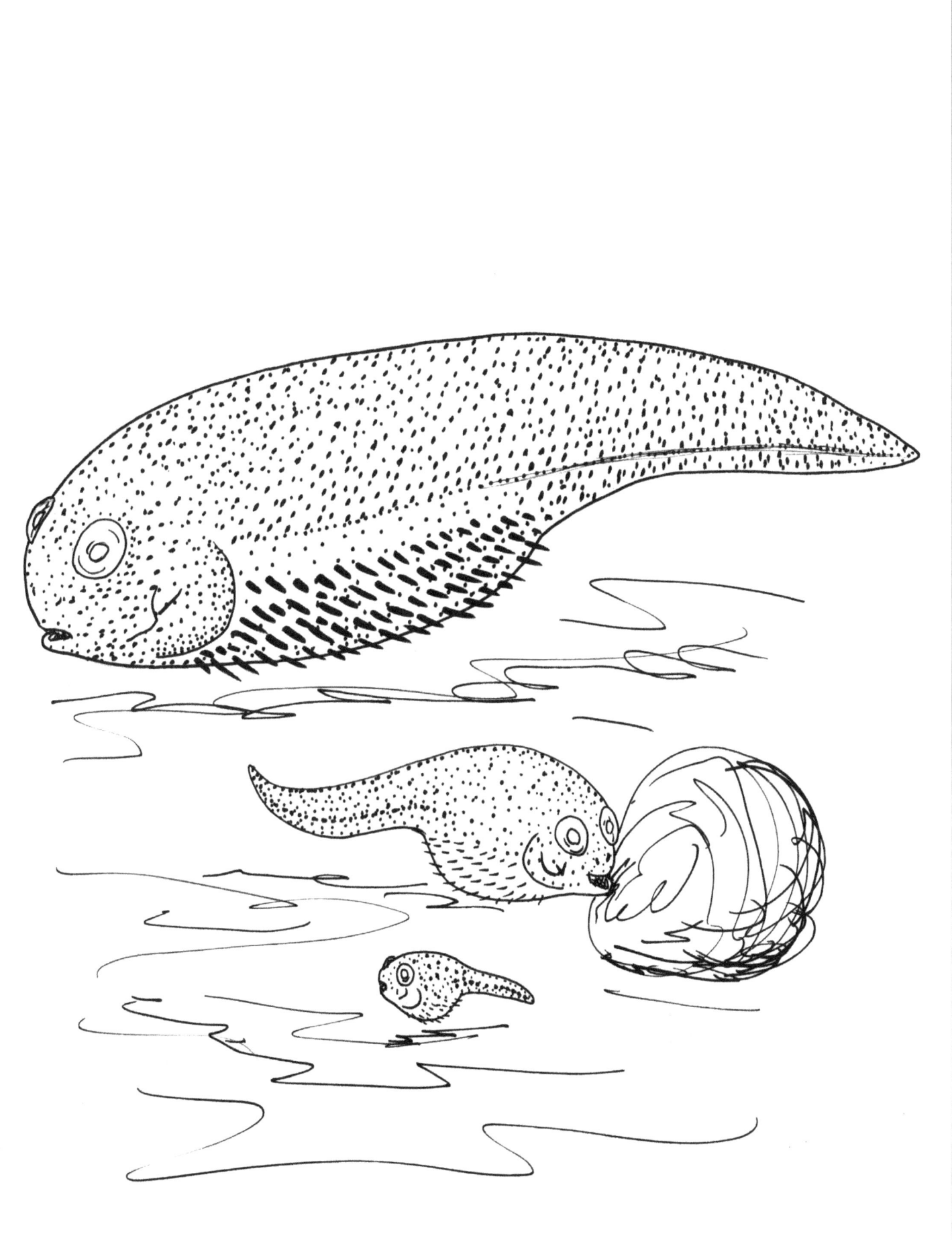

Name	Porcupine Shark
Species	*Listracanthus hystrix*
Phylum	Chordata
Class	Chondrichthyes
Order	*incertae sedis*
Size	Unknown
Time Period	Late Carboniferous until the Early Triassic, from 326 to 251 million years ago
Location	Worldwide
Comments	

The Porcupine Shark, or Porcupine Eel Shark, *Listracanthus hystrix*, which may or may not have been a "shark" shark, is a mysterious cartilaginous fish known exclusively from enormous, comb-like or feather-like spines that appear to have been derived from shagreen-like scales that are found in pile-like arrangements in marine strata dating from the Late Carboniferous until just after the start of the Triassic period.

What the porcupine shark would have looked like is anybody's guess. Professional fish artist, Ray Troll, reconstructed the porcupine shark as looking like a gigantic frill shark-like creature, and justified his reconstruction with a big fish story told to him by palaeoichthyologist Rainer Zangerl. While searching for fossils in a shale quarry in Nevada, Zangerl discovered a fossil of a large, shark-like creature with long spines suggestive of *Listracanthus* spines. Tragically, that fossil disintegrated before it could be brought to a laboratory for examination or preservation (a situation more common than one would think).

Mr Troll's example is followed here, where *L. hystrix* is reconstructed as a large, elongated animal, compared to the shark-like holocephalids *Agassizodus variabilis*, and *Romerodus orodontus* .

Name	Seefeld Lizardsturgeon
Species	*Saurichthys seefeldensis*
Phylum	Chordata
Class	Actinopterygii
Order	Saurichthyiformes
Family	Saurichthyidae
Size	Up to 100 centimeters in length
Time Period	Norian Epoch of the Late Triassic, about 230 to 228 million years ago
Location	Alps of Central Europe, including the Seefeld Formation of Austria
Comments	The Lizardsturgeons of *Saurichthys* is a widespread genus of extinct relatives of the paddlefish and true sturgeons found in marine and freshwater environments throughout the coastal margines of the supercontinent of Pangaea during the Triassic Period. Fossils of lizardsturgeons are found in Triassic-aged strata of Australia, Europe, China, Africa and the Americas. Lizardsturgeons had long, thin beaks similar to the unrelated gars, and the saury fishes, and were probably swift, lurking predators that ambushed unsuspecting prey.

The Seefeld lizardsturgeon, *S. seefeldensis*, lived in estuaries, lagoons and coastal areas an arm of the Tethys Ocean that is now the European Alps. Boluses, balls of undigested bones coughed up, similar to the "owl pellets" of owls, suggest that the lizardsturgeons may have ate small pterosaurs, such as *Preondactylus bufarinii*, as depicted in the picture.

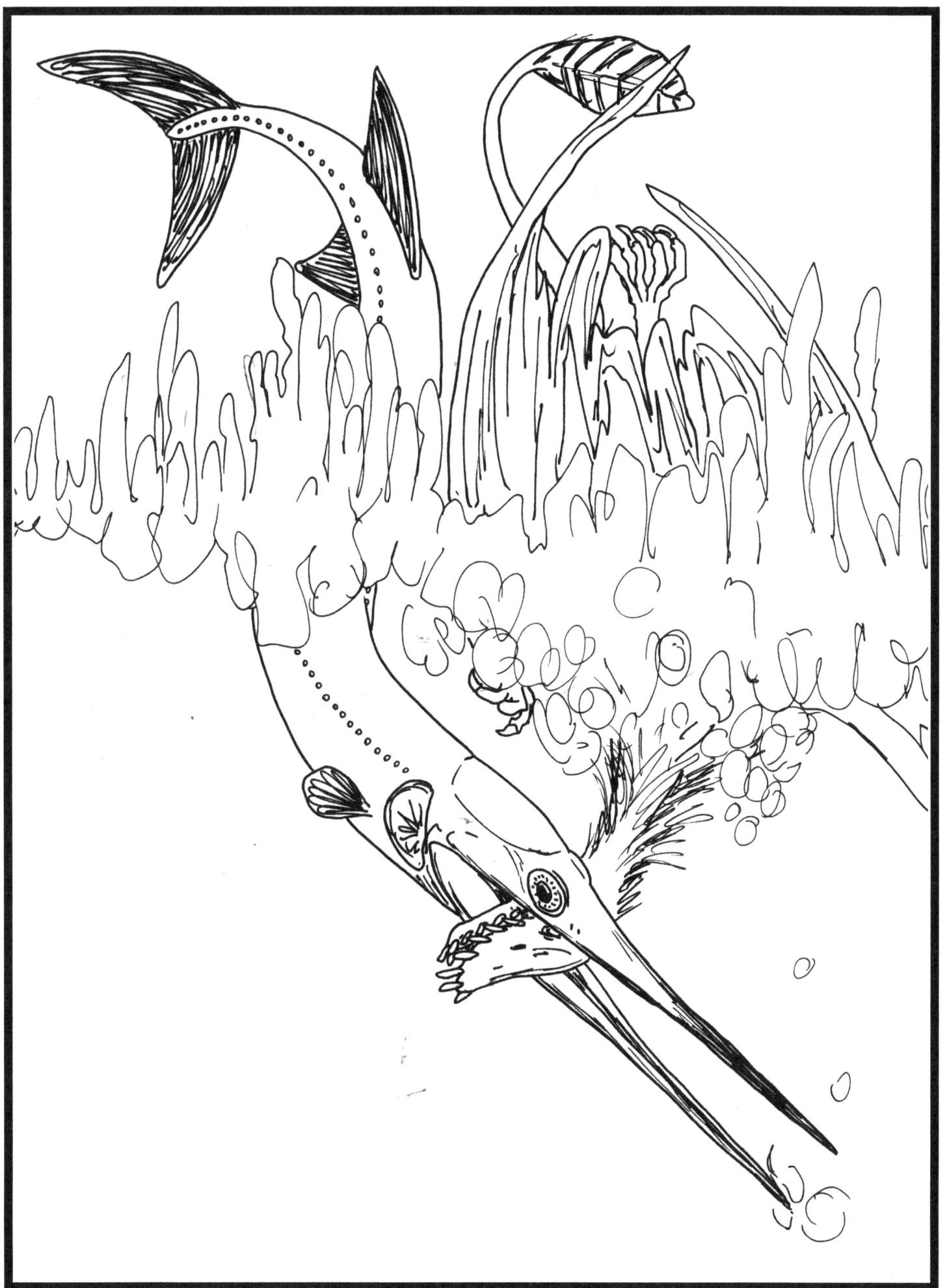

Name	Helmet Anchovy
Species	*Leptolepis coryphaenoides*
Phylum	Chordata
Class	Actinopterygii
Order	Leptolepiformes
Family	Leptolepidae
Size	Up to 30 centimeters in length
Time Period	Kimmeridgian Epoch of the Late Jurassic Period, 155 to 152 million years ago
Location	Bavaria, Germany
Comments	The Helmet Anchovy, *Leptolepis coryphaenoides*, is not closely related to modern-day anchovies of the family Engraulidae. Instead, it is a primitive ray-finned fish more closely related to modern-day gars and bowfins. The helmet anchovy belongs to the genus *Leptolepis,* a long-lived genus that temporally spans from the Middle Triassic until the last species' disappearance from the fossil record during the Early Cretaceous. *Leptolepis* is significant in that, in addition to being a 130 million year long, worldwide dynasty with representatives found in 4 out of the 6 continents, its species are the first bony fishes whose vertebrae are confirmed to be made out of bone tissue, rather than cartilage. In the helmet anchovy's case, its fossils are found in marine limestones of Bavaria, Germany, when the region was a lonely archipelago in the northern edge of the Tethys Ocean. While the helmet anchovy was not related to anchovies, it probably had a very similar lifestyle of swimming in open waters of the ocean, filtering zooplankton out of each swallowed mouthful of water.

Name	Lebanese Helmetfish
Species	*Corusichthys megacephalos*
Phylum	Chordata
Class	Actinopterygii
Order	Pycnodontida
Superfamily	Coccodontoidea
Family	Coccodontidae
Size	Holotype specimen is 3.4 centimeters long.
Time Period	Early Cenomanian Epoch of the Early Cretaceous, about 100 million years ago.
Location	Haqel, Lebanon
Comments	The Lebanese, or Bigheaded Helmetfish, *Corusichthys megacephalos*, is a member of Coccodontoidea, a diverse group of pycnodontid fishes that lived in coral reefs in what is now Lebanon. Many of the Coccodontoids were, like other pycnodontids, big-toothed munchers that nibbled on shellfish and coral, though, some evolved into bizarre forms that continue to confound palaeoichthyologists. The Lebanese helmetfish was one of the more conventional shellfish-nibblers, though, its only known fossil so far shows it was a tiny animal that probably ate very small crustaceans, or very small snails.

# Name	# Lebanese Goblin Shark
Species	*Scapanorhynchus lewisi*
Phylum	Chordata
Class	Chondrichthyes
Subclass	Elasmobranchii
Order	Lamniformes
Family	Mitsukurinidae
Size	Average of 65 centimeters in length
Time Period	Early Cenomanian Epoch of the Early Cretaceous, about 100 million years ago.
Location	Sahel Alma, Lebanon
Comments	The Lebanese Goblin Shark, *Scapanorhynchus lewisi*, is one of several species of (mostly) Cretaceous-aged extinct sharks closely related to the modern-day goblin shark, *Mitsukurina owstoni*. While the awl-shaped teeth of both genera are extremely similar, bordering on identical, goblins of the genus *Scapanorhynchus* tend to have more slender bodies than those of the goblins of *Mitsukurina*. This similarity lead some researchers to assume both were the same genus, though, today, scientific concensus is that both are distinct genera.

Like the modern goblin shark, the Lebanese goblin had a long, elongated snout filled with organs called the "ampullae of Lorenzini," special, nerve-filled pits that allow sharks to detect the bio-electric fields emitted by the nervous systems of other animals. Prey detected this way would be snapped up by the goblin's extendable, extrudable jaws. These jaws caused a number of problems for paleontologists, as so many different specimens of the Lebanese goblin shark have been found, leading researchers to assume that each specimen with a specific degree of jaw extension was a different species.

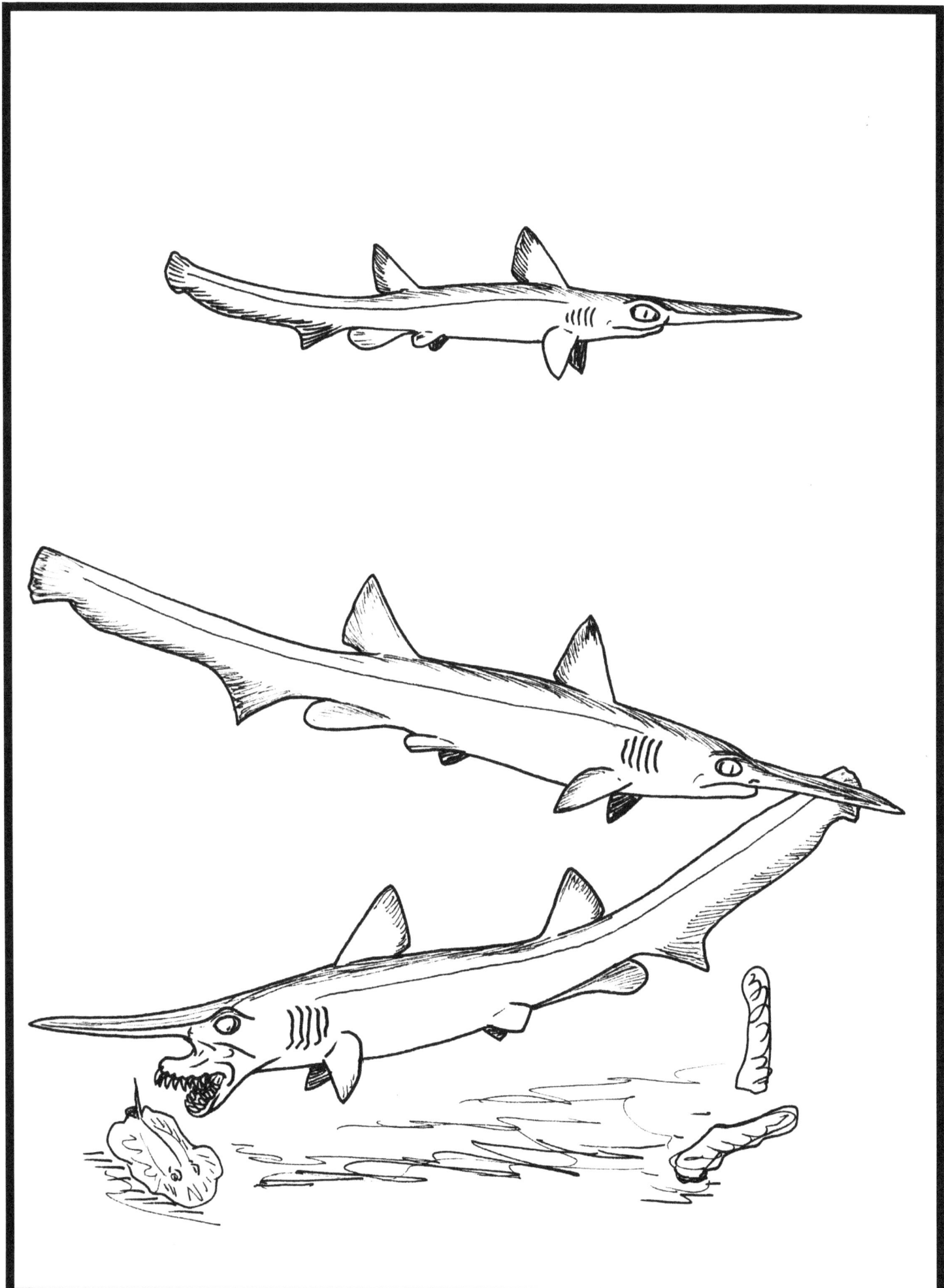

Name	(Robert) Purdy's Moonfish
Species	*Mene purdyi*
Phylum	Chordata
Class	Actinopterygii
Order	Percomorpha
Family	Menidae
Size	Incomplete skull about 8 centimeters in length, body length estimated to be over 40 centimeters
Time Period	Late Thanetian Epoch of the Late Paleocene, 58 to 59 million years ago
Location	"The Mancora Formation of Northwestern Peru, south of Negritos (Lagunitos?)"
Comments	(Robert) Purdy's Moonfish, *Mene purdyi,* shown here with the much smaller modern-day moonfish, *M. maculata*, is the oldest confirmed moonfish, known by a comparitively enormous (for a moonfish) 8 centimeter skull from the Late Paleocene of Peru. The Tunisian, or Phosphate Moonfish, *M. phosphatica*, may date from the Early Paleocene, or it may day from the Early Eocene.

Today, moonfish are reef- and estuary-dwelling animals found throughout the Indo-Pacific, feeding on zooplankton near the substrate in shallow water. The Purdy's moonfish, by contrast, lived in open water away from the coastline, though it, too, most likely also fed on zooplankton.

Name	Rhomboid Moonfish
Species	*Mene rhombea*
Phylum	Chordata
Class	Actinopterygii
Order	Percomorpha
Family	Menidae
Size	Body length up to 10 centimeters, up to 30 centimeters with pelvic fins.
Time Period	Lutetian Epoch of the Middle Eocene, from 48 to 40 million years ago.
Location	Monte Bolca, Italy
Comments	The Rhomboid Moonfish, *Mene rhombea*, is one of the most iconic of the Monte Bolca lagerstätte, and is, ironically, probably the best-studied of all the species in the genus *Mene*, even more studied than the living moonfish, *M. maculata*.

During the Eocene and Oligocene, Italy was a series of volcanic islands surrounded by coral reefs. During the Lutetian, the reef where Monte Bolca is now held an extremely diverse fish community.

Much like *M. maculata*, the rhomboid moonfish lived near the substrate of the shallower regions of Monte Bolca's reef, nibbling and filterfeeding on zooplankton. In the picture, the larger rhomboid is compared to the other moonfish of Monte Bolca, the oblong moonfish, *M. oblonga*. Ironically, the oblong moonfish would survive into the early Oligocene, where it is known from a single fossil found in what is now Chiavon, Italy. |

Name	Iranian Hedgehogfish
Species	*Iraniplectus bakhtiari*
Phylum	Chordata
Class	Actinopterygii
Order	Tetraodontiformes
Family	Zignoichthyidae
Size	About 14 centimeters long
Time Period	Rupelian Epoch of the Oligocene Period, 34 to 28 million years ago
Location	Zagros Mountains near Baba Heydar, Western Iran.
Comments	The Iranian Hedgehogfish, *Iraniplectus bakhtiari*, is an extinct member of the Pufferfish Order, Tetraodontiformes, and, together with its Italian Eocene relative, Zigno's Oblong, *Zignoichthys oblongus*, represent a stage in Tetraodontiform evolution where the pelvis and pelvic fins were lost, transitioning between the Threetooth Puffer and its extinct relatives (*Triodon* of Triodontidae), and the true puffers, porcupine fish and ocean sunfish (Tetraodontidae, Diodontidae and Molidae, respectively).

One of the most noticeable features of the Iranian hedgehogfish is its covering of star-shaped scales. In life, the hedgehogfish would have looked very much like a porcupine fish with a sagging, floppy belly. Because it had beak-like teeth typical to most tetraodontiform fishes, the hedgehogfish probably preyed on small shellfish.

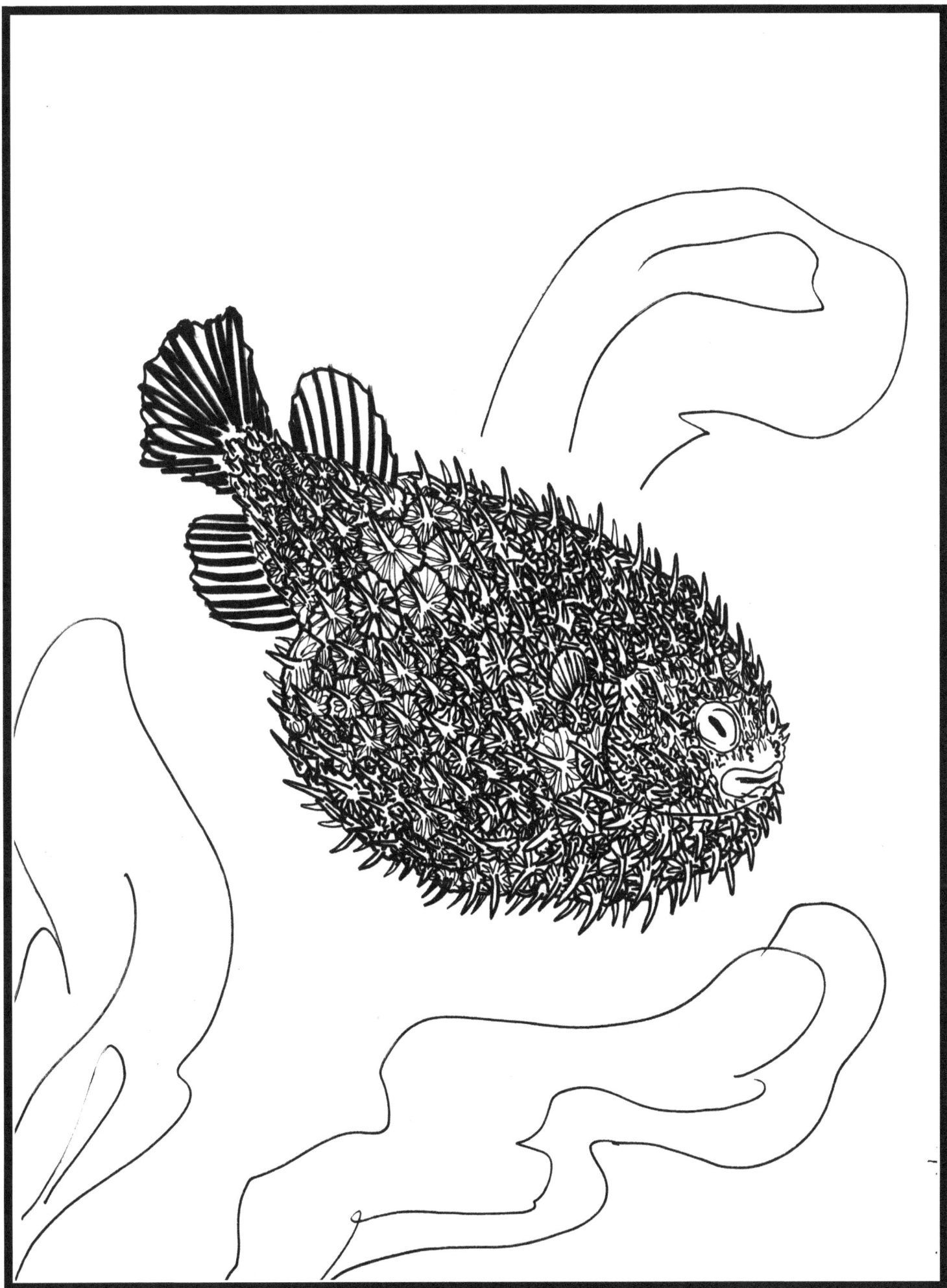

Name	Suzurisaba
Species	*Polymerichthys nagurai*
Phylum	Chordata
Class	Actinopterygii
Order	Aulopiformes
Suborder	Alepisauroidea
Family	Polymerichthyidae
Size	Longest specimen about 17 centimeters long
Time Period	Late Oligocene to Middle Miocene, probably 25 to 12 million years ago
Location	Sakhalin Island (Oligocene), Italy and Tubozawa Formation, Horaiji, Aichi Prefecture, Japan (Middle Miocene)
Comments	The Suzurisaba, or Inkstone Mackerel, *Polymerichthys nagurai*, is an extinct, eel-like aulopiform fish closely related to the lancetfishes of *Alepisaurus*, (in the background of the picture) and the daggertooths of *Anotopterus*, and possibly represents a transition between the two.

The first specimen was discovered by an inkstone or suzuri maker, Masayasu Nagurai, in 1927, in the Aichi Prefecture in Honshu, Japan. Later, Nagurai-san donated his find to the National Science Museum in Tokyo, where it would be studied.

In addition to Japan, a fragment of a skull was found in similar-aged Miocene rocks in Italy, and recently, several specimens were found in Late Oligocene-aged rocks in Sakhalin Island. The Sakhalin specimens may hint at sexual dimorphism.

The long head with long teeth easily demonstrate that the suzurisaba had a predatory lifestyle.

Name   Qaidam Snowtrout

Species   *Hsianwenia wuii*

Phylum   Chordata

Class   Actinopterygii

Order   Cypriniformes

Family   Cyprinidae

Subfamily   Barbinae

Tribe   Schizothoracini

Size   Estimated to be up to 50 centimeters long

Time Period Pliocene

Location   Upper portion of the Shizigou Formation in the Yahu Anticline, of the Qaidam Basin in the northern portion of the Tibetan Plateau.

Comments   The Qaidam Snowtrout, *Hsianwenia wuii*, whose scientific name commemorates one Professor Hsianwen Wui, an important scientist crucial in helping to understand living cyprinid fishes of China, is an extinct relative of the living snowtrout cyprinids of *Schizothorax* and *Ptychobarbus*.

During the Miocene, the Qaidam Basin was a freshwater lake in what is now the Tibetan Plateau. As the Indian Plate continued to press against the Eurasian Plate, thereby continue uplifting the region, this lake began drying out. During the Pliocene, the lake's water became very briny and laden with calcium carbonates. The Qaidam snowtrout evolved to adapt to this environment toxically oversaturated with calcium carbonate via the process of pachyostosis, in that the animal sequestered extra calcium carbonates by developing extra-thick ribs. Because no specimens below 40 centimeters have been found, researchers suspect that the animals did not develop these thickened, hypercalcified ribs until they were fully grown (probably around age 8 or 10 years according to living snowtrouts).

Name   Sabertooth Salmon

Species   *Onchorhynchus rastrosus*

Phylum   Chordata

Class   Actinopterygii

Order   Salmoniformes

Family   Salmonidae

Size   Up to 270 centimeters in length

Time Period   Late Miocene to Early Pleistocene, 6 to about 2 million years ago

Location   Pacific coast of North America, from Southern Alaska to Southern California.

Comments   The Sabertooth Salmon, *Onchorhynchus rastrosus*, is the largest known salmons ever to exist, with males estimated to be up to 270 centimeters long. The sabertooth salmon's fossils are found in Middle to Late Neogene-aged freshwater strata all along the Pacific Coast of North America from San Bernadino County, California up to Southern Alaska. These fossils are of adults who, much like other ocean-going species of *Onchorhynchus*, died of exhaustion after swimming upstream to mate and lay eggs.

The "sabertooth" of the sabertooth salmon refers to the two spine-like teeth emanating from the tip of the snout of adult males. Unlike mammalian sabertooths, or other species of *Onchorhynchus*,.the sabertooth salmon had only a few teeth at the tips of their jaws, and none of these teeth were used in grasping prey. This feature, together with proportionally larger gills lead researchers to believe the adult sabertooth salmon was a planktivore.

In the picture, the sabertooth salmon are swimming upstream, and are encountering their lake-dwelling relative, the Idaho Rhabdofario, *O. lacustris*, which lived in lakes of the Pacific Northwest of the U.S.A. from the late Miocene until before the start of the first Pleistocene Ice Ages.

Name	Amanto
Species	*Orestias cuvieri*
Phylum	Chordata
Class	Mammalia
Order	Cyprinidontiformes
Family	Cyprinidontidae
Tribe	Orestiini
Size	Maximum recorded length 22 centimeters
Time Period	Last seen during the 1930's
Location	Lake Titicaca, between Peru and Boliva

Comments

The Amanto, Umautos, or Lake Titicaca Orestias, *Orestias cuvieri*, is an extinct species of pupfish endemic to deep water of Lake Titicaca. The young were called "Peje Rey," and should not be confused with the South American silverside of *Odontesthes*, which are called "pejerrey." The amanto was easily distinguished from all other pupfish in general by its enormous, box-like head and upturned, almost vertical mouth. The peje rey was silver-gray, with fins that had black bands. Upon adulthood, the amanto was a greyed, dingy yellow chartreuse, more yellow on the dorsal side, and more gray-umber on the belly. The adult male, who was smaller than the female, had hints of orange during mating season. Both adult and juveniles ate planktonic crustaceans.

The amanto and all other members of *Orestias* are descended from the Loja pupfish, *Carionellus diumortuus*, from Early Miocene Loja, Ecuador.

While the amanto has been fished by humans since Titicaca's shores have been inhabited, the amanto's doom began in the 19th Century, when Europeans began introducing exotic fish species, primarily trout, such as the lake trout, *Salvelinus namaycush*, shown here, and pejerrey, into the lake in order to create more "productive fisheries." Unsurprisingly, these alien predators preyed all of the indigenous animals, making the amanto extremely rare; by the 1930s, people caught very few, if any at all. Fish census surveys from 1962 onward have failed to find any amanto. Industrial and agricultural pollution probably finished off the amanto, as Lake Titicaca has become very polluted during the 20th and 21st Centuries, with frequent die-offs becoming a very sad norm there.

Bibliography

- Arratia, Gloria. "Reassessment of the phylogenetic relationships of certain Jurassic teleosts and their implications on teleostean phylogeny." *Mesozoic fishes—systematics and paleoecology* (1996): 219-242.
- Arratia, Gloria. "Leptolepis, Paraleptolepis (Teleostei) and a new fish name." *Mitteilungen aus dem Museum für Naturkunde, Berlin, Geowissenschaftliche Reihe* 6 (2003): 157-159.
- Cavender, Ted M., and Robert Rush Miller. "Smilodonichthys rastrosus a new Pliocene salmonid fish from western United States." (1972).
- Chang, Meemann, et al. "Extraordinarily thick-boned fish linked to the aridification of the Qaidam Basin (northern Tibetan Plateau)." *Proceedings of the National Academy of Sciences* 105.36 (2008): 13246-13251.
- Costa, W. J. E. M. "Redescription and phylogenetic position of the fossil killifish† *Carrionellus diumortuus* White from the Lower Miocene of Ecuador (Teleostei: Cyprinodontiformes)." *Cybium* 35.3 (2011): 181-7.
- Day, David. The doomsday book of animals: a natural history of vanished species. Penguin Putnam, 1981.
- Frickhinger, Karl Albert Fossilien Atlas Fische, Mergus-Verlag, Melle, 1999
- Friedman, Matt, and G. David Johnson. "A new species of Mene (Perciformes: Menidae) from the Paleocene of South America, with notes on paleoenvironment and a brief review of menid fishes." *Journal of Vertebrate Paleontology* 25.4 (2005): 770-783.
- Gagnier, P. Y., and A. Blieck. "On Sacabambaspis janvieri and the vertebrate diversity in Ordovician seas." *Mark-Kurik E In Fossil fishes as living animals Academia* 1 (1992): 9-20.
- Janvier, Philippe. (1993). Patterns of diversity in the skull of jawless fishes. In *The Skull* (ed. J. Hanken and B. K. Hall), Vol. 2, pp. 131–188. The University of Chicago Press.
- Janvier, Philippe. 1996, 2003. Early Vertebrates (1996); Early Vertebrates (2003). Oxford Monographs on Geology and Geophysics, v. 33, Oxford University Press, Oxford, England, ISBN 978-0-19-854047-2
- Long, John A. The Rise of Fishes: 500 Million Years of Evolution. Baltimore: The Johns Hopkins University Press, 1996
- Nazarkin, Mikhail V. "Cenozoic fossil fishes of the extinct alepisauroid family Polymerichthyidae from the Sakhalin Island, Russia." *ACTA PALAEONTOLOGICA POLONICA* 61.4 (2016): 829-838.
- Parenti, Lynne R. A taxonomic revision of the Andean killifish genus *Orestias* (Cyprinodontiformes, Cyprinodontidae). American museum of natural history, 1984.
- Pradel, Alan, et al. "The tail of the Ordovician fish Sacabambaspis." *Biology letters* 3.1 (2007): 73-76.
- Saller, Franco, Silvio Renesto, and Fabio M. Dalla Vecchia. "First record of Langobardisaurus (Diapsida, Protorosauria) from the Norian (Late Triassic) of Austria,

and a revision of the genus." *Neues Jahrbuch für Geologie und Paläontologie-Abhandlungen* 268.1 (2013): 83-95.

- Shu, Degan G., et al. "Lower Cambrian vertebrates from south China." *Nature* 402.6757 (1999): 42-46.

- Shu, D-G., et al. "Head and backbone of the Early Cambrian vertebrate Haikouichthys." *Nature* 421.6922 (2003): 526-529.

- Taverne, L., Capasso, L. (2014). "Ostéologie et phylogénie des Coccodontidae, une famille remarquable de poissons Pycnodontiformes du Crétacé supérieur marin du Liban, avec la description de deux nouveaux genres". Palaeontos. 25

- Troll, Ray. Sharkabet: A Sea of Sharks from A to Z. WestWinds Press, 2002.

- Tyler, JAMES C., M. A. J. I. D. Mirzaie, and A. L. I. R. E. Z. A. Nazemi. "New genus and species of basal tetraodontoid puffer fish from the Oligocene of Iran, related to the Zignoichthyidae (Tetraodontiformes)." *Bollettino del Museo Civico di Storia Naturale di Verona* 30 (2006): 49-58.

- Uyeno, Teruya. "A Miocene alepisauroid fish of a new family, Polymerichthyidae, from Japan." *Bull. Nat. Sci. Mus* 10 (1967): 383-394.

- Wallace, David Rains. *Neptune's ark: from ichthyosaurs to orcas*. Univ of California Press, 2007.

- Zhu, Min, et al. "A Silurian maxillate placoderm illuminates jaw evolution." *Science* 354.6310 (2016): 334-336.

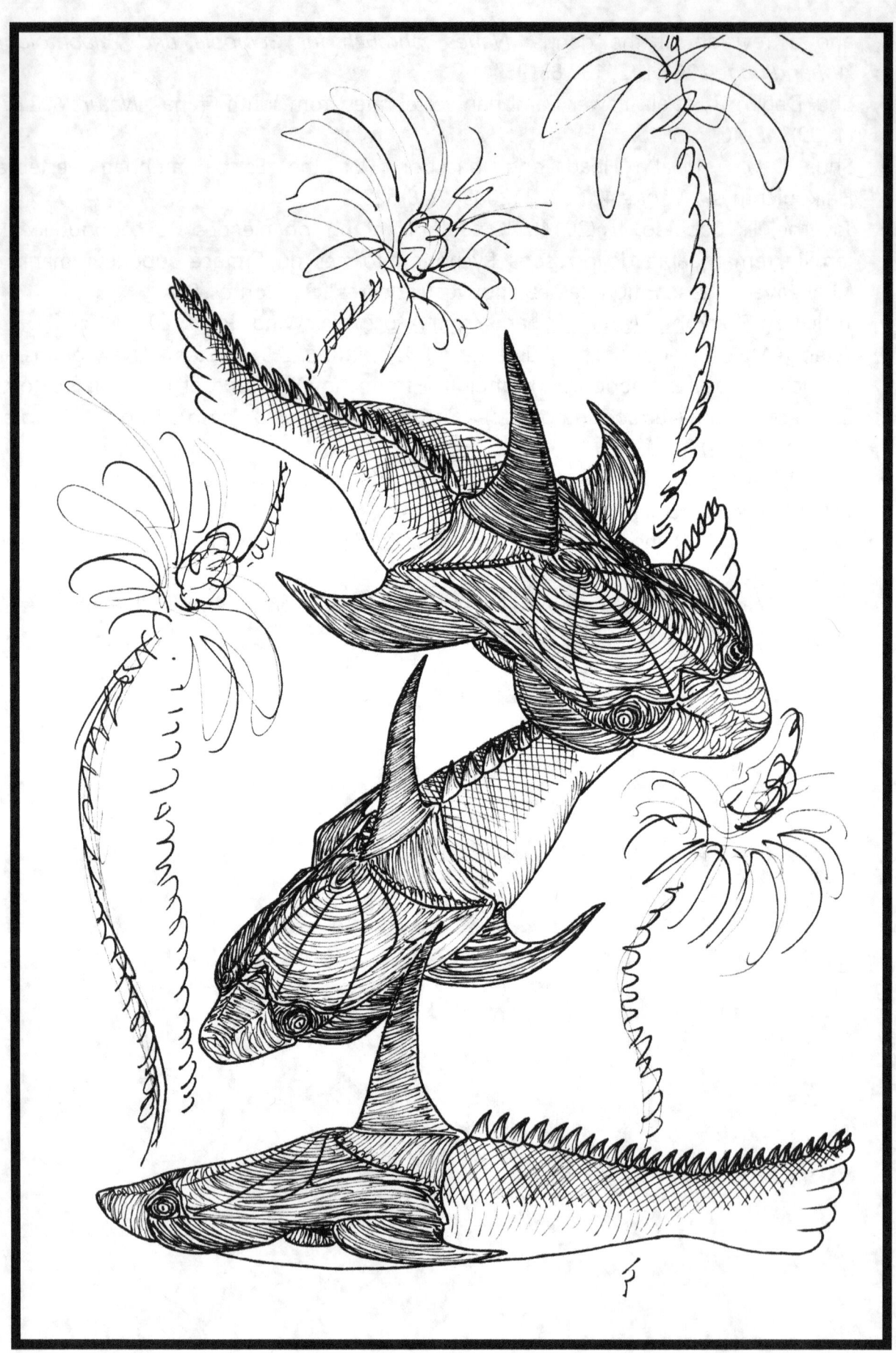

About the Artist

Stanton F. Fink is a student of Biology and Chinese Medicine, and makes a hobby of drawing monsters and researching flowers, arcane-looking creatures, prehistoric animals, fish, reptiles, birds and the occasional, really grotesque fungal fruiting body.

Stanton grew up and went to school in California and is currently living, drawing, and gardening in Oregon.